OPEN FIST
An Anthology Of Young Illinois Poets

EDITED BY
Anne Schultz

TIA CHUCHA PRESS
CHICAGO

Special thanks to Olga Avalos, who was indispensable to the production of this book, and to poets Eugene Redmond of East St. Louis, Kim Berez of Chicago and Michael Warr for helping us contact the young people. Thanks to John Starrs and Zoe Keithley of the Chicago Teachers' Center for helping with the interviews, and Jackie Murphy for accommodating Olga while she worked on the manuscript. And a big thanks to all the young poets who contributed work: although we could only use a few, all of you conveyed the same spirit and power of expressive language represented in this book.

Cover art: Detail from a painting by Dzine
Book design: Jane Brunette Kremsreiter
Photography: Diana Solis. Photo of Francesca Abbate by C. Lyman.

ISBN 1-882688-01-5

Library of Congress Catalog Number: 93-60983

Tia Chucha Press
A project of the Guild Complex
PO Box 476969
Chicago IL 60647

This project was partially supported by grants from the National Endowment for the Arts, the Illinois Arts Council, and Chicago's Department of Cultural Affairs. Special thanks to the Lannan Foundation for a grant to publicize this and other Tia Chucha books.

CONTENTS

PREFACE

Voices angry, voices gentle, voices tender, voices violent, voices declaring, yearning, fighting, lusting, hurting, confronting, hoping, and loving; voices confused, sharp, clear, passionate, precise, demanding, and worthy of being heard. Voices painting pictures, telling stories, taking us into their hearts.

A few years ago at a small summer theater in the Berkshires, I saw a play that Chekhov had written when he was sixteen. It was wonderful to see the seeds of what would later become his genius, and I thought rather sadly about how infrequently we witness artists' work in the particular passion of youth, before their voices are fully formed. The talented young voices in this book are still emerging. It is just because of this that they speak not only for themselves but for young people everywhere.

These poets are exhilarating in their differences, both cultural and individual. But finally it is their similarities that are more important, and perhaps this is the main celebration of this anthology. They're "out there," wherever out there is, and they're there together, with all of their disparate backgrounds and experiences. They are America, these young voices, a young America which shows itself clearly in these poems to care deeply and to have a compassionate conscience—to be doing its damnedest to live decently against what sometimes seems to be overwhelming odds. Their poems testify to, and are in the service of, this living. Writing poetry is their breath and their necessity. They shape the experience of being young in America in 1993 into the words and music they have inside them which speaks on behalf of us all.

On the main entrance of every Chicago public school is written: "Our Children . . . Our Future." These young poets are our future because they are also our present and a reminder of, and a link to, our past.

Editing this book has been an honor and a privilege. It has been both rewarding and moving to meet these gifted young people, to see their work in all its vibrancy and seriousness of purpose. Perhaps the world isn't in such bad shape after all.

Salute and enjoy Andrea, Claire, Danica, Eduardo, Francesca, Jeanette, Luis, Ramiro, Salem and Vu Dang. I am proud to offer you Tia Chucha's young poets.

Anne Schultz

DANICA CHO

Danica Cho is seventeen and was born and raised in Chicago. Her mother is from South Korea and came to the United States with her mother (Danica's grandmother).

Danica likes to read political and social poetry in which people express their struggle: poets from the Vietnam war; former drug addicts; people who spent time in jail. "When a line goes straight to my heart and I feel I know exactly what that person was feeling, it gives me a thrill." The main purpose of poetry for her is to be able to express what she feels, to get it out. A few years ago she was very lonely and cried almost every day—it was all bottled up inside her. "It's bad to bottle it up," she says, and is moved now when poets write of loneliness. She's not in that place any more, but she remembers.

She writes in response to things that happen to her, particularly when she's angry or depressed. When people upset her, she finds it hard to talk back to them. "I lash it all out in my poetry. It gives my feelings some kind of shape and form."

ARTHRITIC ARCTIC

i stole an orchid from the altar
           the other day

i brushed my face against its soft petals and smiled
remembering the silky smoothness of your skin . . .
like creamy white chocolate
the way you say my name like a sweet caress
your smile promising of a warm summer morning
and i, cradling in the warmth of your eyes.
but when i carefully approached you today
with quivering lips and sweaty hands
and bestowed you with this orchid
cultivated by dreams—
                    TIME FROZE
all at once i could smell an ugly, blistering winter
sneaking up from behind me
my arthritic heart began to shake
swelling with pain
throbbing off-beat
against the rhythm of your laughter—
slashing me
drawing icicles of blood
and i could feel my voice crack like shattered ice
as i lost my footing
and slipped
on the icy stairs to your heart.

SAM I AM

slouched in a wooden chair
gazing past the distant, barred windows
amidst dim lights
stale smoke of cheap cigarettes
low hum of a pink glow from
a coughing neon sign

you okay, sam? Chang asks
wiping away at
the dingy counter
riddled
with cries
from thick black pungent markers
branding desperate pleas to be remembered
by this frost-bitten world

what'll it be, sam? Chang asks

as he turns
flashing yellow teeth under his
foul breath
i know he's been sneaking in the back
again
sitting atop a broken icy toilet
stuffing sour soy sauce and acrid kim-chee into his
rotten mouth
with those chipped bamboo chopsticks he keeps
in the stained pocket of his
flimsy
white shirt

TUB OF HOT COCOA, AND DON'T SKIMP ON THE MARSHMAL-
LOWS

okee-dokee, sam

my palms embrace the warmth of the styrofoam cup
steam kissing my lips
like a two-timing gigolo
it lingers
teasing
then disappears into the frigid air
without a trace . . .
i didn't even get his name . . .

helplessly stranded in this choking pit
the crummy jukebox in the dark dusty corner
waits to be fed sacrificed quarters by
heartbroken fools
like me;

sing dem blues wid me, babe

something about a slow swayin' song
that wails along with a crying heart—
a tender duet—-
playing old clips of memories
muted in my mind
reminding me of that soft July night
i on your front steps
as you lay stretched out on the porch swing
a contented cat,
oblivious . . .
lazily basking in moonlit rays
unconscious of the starry eyes
mesmerized by you . . .

no!
stop!
i can't take it anymore!!!
guzzling forcefully
hot cocoa scalds my tongue
i storm out
forgetting my coat
knowing that Chang calls everybody

sam.

SUPERSTAR

that sticky summer in Goshen
between the home-made ice cream
nights of laughter beside a burning candle
damn blood-sucking vampire mosquitoes
his signature always read:
Nat Jordan, SUPERSTAR

he looked at me
with affection
with blue-grey eyes
and thin red lips
and as he stood there
that Sunday morning
struggling to bury his tears
amidst worn-out Bibles
below-the-knee dresses
cloroxed dress shirts
virgin and indifferent hearts
his quavering voice declared

IT'S SO EASY TO LOVE THE LORD

i wanted to run
bolt out,
escape
to anywhere
but especially to him
cry in his arms
he was so . . .

beautiful.

I WANT TO SEE BLOOD

you thought i was
a nobody
you'd rather
comb your terrier
watch shao-lin monks on your
damn tv
pick the scuzz off
between your teeth
than tell me over the
phone—
my sustaining umbilical cord—
that you know
i exist.

every moon that passed
my pillow was
drenched
with tears
my face
a mask of play-dough
so tired
from screaming
worn out from the merciless
digging of your cold,
blunt fingers
muffling wrenching sobs

but then
you discovered
i wasn't just the
plain
ordinary
invisible
no one

after all.
you look at me now
at a distance
staring
with eyes different
not your own
when you stand before me
your eyes are cast on the dirt floor
stammering
not knowing
where to start
the words caught in your throat
as i'm plastering
brick upon brick
the wall of knotted tension
between us
laughing
my vengeful eyes
glaring
thundering
shrieking
BLOOD! BLOOD!
I WANT TO SEE BLOOD!
your shrieks and crunching bones
go unheeded
by my blinded ears
as i gather you up in the
palm of my bony hand
and crush you
tasteless
flat . . .
grinning
because i can feel the
cool pulp of your
dead flesh
against the
hot
metal sheet of my skin

and seeing your blood
oozing
from the shafts of my iron knuckles
mixing
with the brown rust
formed from my tears
i am
satisfied.

WITH THE WIND IN OUR HAIR

with the wind in our hair
and our book bags as goal posts
we played roller hockey at Diversey Harbor
until the great tangerine ball dipped
across the toothpick masts
and you told me how you cried
before i had discovered you.
it was such a sad song, you moaned
staring down at the black asphalt.

i had cried a sad song.
i wanted to tell you

i think

as we waded our sore feet in the icy waters
off the shore of Oak Street Beach
the skyline behind us against
a splash of midnight blue
illuminated by the city lights like
the stars in your eyes that i knew you were hiding from me
behind the wall
of your long blond bangs;
the waves pulled and teased beneath my feet
a warning to the fool who built his foundation on sand
instead of rock
remembering the nights i spent
tossing and turning in fits of frustration
yearning for true kisses and loving hands
shrieking with hammering fists to break free from
this belt of chastity—gnawing, twisting, choking me
to a grave of guilt.
and now i had you between my thumb and index finger
though we were mirrored images of flat paper dolls in a

                    black and white
                         movie
and i was the director
frantically debating whether or not i should scream out
CUT!!!
because i knew you wanted me
to wrap myself around you and hold you tight
hiss poisonous lies of I LOVE YOU in your ear
and shove my forked tongue down your throat—

but instead i waited
for your dad to drive us home
and eat Arby's curly q's in silence
with the windows rolled down
and the wind in our hair.

LAWRENCE AND WESTERN

Feed me
Feed me
it growls
as he rides on its back
a flea on a bandit dog

Jonah's
huddled on a corner
waiting impatiently for the whale
to swallow them,
save them from
the bitter attack
of the icy morning—
REPENT
BEFORE IT'S TOO LATE—
they wrinkle their noses at the
putrid stench
of the open can of
bait
composed of
crushed Pepsi cans
Styrofoam coffee cups
half-eaten what-nots

the flea
clutches the can of bait
his veins heaving,
contracting,
pulling back,
back,
finally surrendering it
into the cold, hard jaws of the
mechanical monster
emanating

shrill beeps
pulsing red lights.
Satisfied,
it drudges on
stuffing itself
till it finally
vomits
and not knowing where to
bury it,
we ourselves are buried
in its
sourly stale
vomit.

KIM·CHEE·FREE

For once, free from my tight-fisted dungeon
of kim-chee and stale sushi
these winding streets of delicious culture
envelop me.
Fuchsia-haired, nose-pierced rebels in
black leather jackets stranded on a corner,
defying and denying
our world of conformity.
Staring past my reflection
through glass walls and dim lights
I violate private chats
over steaming cups of cappucino with
my thirsty eyes
lingering a second too long before they catch me
red-handed,
like snails resenting the hassled peace
provoked from their unforeseen
upturning shelter of rock.

Here, I can feel the hypnotizing beat of an African drum.
Here, I can taste the soft cream of German pastries
      in my mind.
Here, I can breathe in Brazilian coffee beans
      like an opium addict.

And it's then, when i can feel
my dry, brittle toes
slowly curling into the cracks of the sidewalk, that I can
stretch my limbs out to hug the painted sky
and finally be able to say

              "I know where my roots are."

RAMIRO RODRIGUEZ

Ramiro is eighteen years old. He was born in Los Angeles and came to Chicago when he was thirteen. Ramiro looks on writing poetry as a hobby. He wants to be an electrician, not a poet. He enjoys doing it, though; in the wintertime, he generally has his notebook with him, small enough to fit into the pocket of his jacket. But in the summer when he doesn't have his jacket, he doesn't have his notebook either, so the poems don't get written. "If I hadn't had a jacket with a pocket, these poems would never have gotten written," he says.

He can't write for assignment, only when a poem comes to him, and it always comes out differently on the page than it was in his mind. The thoughts and ideas he has—he thinks a lot—and the images he sees are the origins of his poems, but they are not the poems. They are what get him to the paper, but they are not what gets down on the paper. Ramiro writes responsively, one line growing out of the one that came before it. He writes all at once until he's run out of ideas. And it's always quite different from what he was thinking about at the beginning. He doesn't add anything after he's finished; if he were to do so, it would then be another poem.

SWITCHBLADE

See how the blade shines luminously.
From any kind of light.
Look at the jagged edge,
Doesn't it look like teeth
       ready to snap at anybody?
Throw it!
Doesn't it fly rapidly through the air,
Cutting the air as it is about
       to hit the wall?
Right at that point,
It looks like it is
       looking for a target,
Like a psychopath
       looking for his next victim.

Give yourself a deep slash
By this deadly weapon,
Look at it.
It tears away your flesh,
While you scream
       in pain and agony.
The slash looks
       like a pair of lips,
Ready to swallow the germs around you.

This uncaring weapon
       destroys the life and hopes
Of millions of people everyday.
It defends people from life and from themselves.
Look around you and you'll see someone
Switching a blade.
If you want to LIVE
Be careful.
The world is dangerous!

NIGHTMARE

1

So many false hopes.
So many false answers.
Who am I?
What am I?
Did I come into this
world unknown?
Did I come into this
world with a gun in my
hand and a needle up my arm?
Was I born to die,
crying for salvation?
Crying for hope?
Is my pain ever going to
be healed?
Is my hurt ever going to be
noticed?
Walking down a lonely
path into
a lonely world with a
lonely hurt only meant
for me.

2

My life is so confused.
Everywhere I turn
I step into a world of
disillusionment.
Why is my head full of
false dreams and
        hopes?
Now tell me, is it because
of my father?
A father who abandoned me

since I was two.
A father who, 11 years later
decided to finally accept
me.
But my father,
look at what I have become.
Now tell me, is it because
of my mother?
A mother who beat and
punished me for thirteen years,
until I was able to leave to a different
world of horrors.
A mother who four years later
tried to better herself, just
for the love of me.
But my mother, look at what I
have become.
Or is it because of a system?
A system that shaped and
molded these two people into what
they have become.
A system that
tried to destroy their dreams
and hopes a long time ago.
Almighty system, LOOK AT WHAT YOU HAVE MADE ME!!!

3

Being with you
amazes me.
You have your boyfriend,
I have my gang.
But there is an attraction
between us that intertwines
into an everlasting longing
for each other.
Hopefully you will come
to understand that my
feelings for you are

true.
My blood runs with
yours into a river of
ecstasy and pain.
The ecstasy for what's
about to come.
And the pain for what's
about to end.

4

Reality is the death of life.
Reality is a simplicity
that comes and goes,
but never ends.
Who wants to live in a
world full of reality?
Why not live in a world full
of strange and bizarre images?
Where we could fly and
fly and never worry about
people shooting us from
the ground.
Where we could use
our minds for advancement
and technology and never
worry about people telling us
we're stupid.
Where we could fall
asleep into a deep
everlasting dream and never
worry about somebody
trying to wake us up.

5

Look through the eyes
of the innocent and what
do you see?
You see a boy running.

running from family, friends
and LIFE.
Yes, life
where reality seeps through your veins like
a drug
which you can never get rid of no matter
how much it terrorizes your
mind and body and soul.
Sleep child for a new day
is coming.
A new day of pain
                    hurt
                    sorrow
            and of bitterness
                        and despair.
Is this a future to come?
Where innocence is destroyed at
birth.
Where nine and ten year olds are
getting shot by a system
that allows us to kill
each other.
Where nine, ten year olds lose
their virginity to a system
that deplores sex as an act
of violence instead of as an act
of love.
What's to become of our
children? Are we going to
destroy them by our own
hands? Or are we going to
give them a future where
they could hold the
past to their hearts
as an understanding of love
and hatred?   Where they
could learn to upbring the
love and destroy the hatred?

6

Lonely in my gray world.
More of my friends dead,
instead of saved.
Death is our new future.
No colleges for us.
No business suit wearing jobs
for us.
The only college we'll
go to is our hood.
The only business suit
wearing jobs we'll have is
drug-dealing.
These ain't animal
activities to us.
These things are OUR society.
Our way of living.
Our way of dying.
Born in the hood.

                 *

Killed in the hood.
These words are my life now.
I live for what each letter
represents.
It could have been any other
name.
It could have been any other
hood.
But this was the first to
grab me.
The first to hold me in its
seductive power.
The first to feed into my
immaturity.
It taught me.
It nurtured me.

This represents my gang affiliation which should remain nameless.

It gave me a family.
It gave me a need of belonging
It turned me into a man. ALWAYS AND FOREVER.

7

The solution to the
problems of the world is
in our hearts.
We claim we love each
other,
but in actuality we hate
each other.
We have to stop thinking
with our minds and start
thinking with our hearts.
We need to learn to love our children.
We need to learn to love
ourselves.
We need to learn to
embrace the future
and learn from the mistakes
of the past.

SALEM COLLO-JULIN

Salem Collo-Julin is eighteen and was born in Chicago. She is the only child of a Filipino mother and an Irish father. When she was little, her mother used to take her along to her office at least once a week. Salem would sit at a desk with an endless supply of paper and write. She wrote her first poem there.

She especially likes Adrienne Rich's poetry—she is drawn to the strength behind the work. Sometimes she will read only women writers. "I'm doing an injustice to my sex if I don't read women. But then I realize that's only half the world and I want the whole world, so I start to include male authors again." In high school it was William Carlos Williams who turned her around about poetry. Until Salem read him, she thought people wrote poetry only because they didn't have enough to say to write a story. "He was the first poet I read who was into the image for the sake of itself. This opened up a whole new world for me," she says.

Her parents have always been very supportive of her as a writer. "They're happy that I've found something that I love to do, and they are very encouraging."

BLUE

when we found the ocean
she was more blue than I imagined
an ancient song hidden in her curves
I danced on the shore, lifting arms to the infinite breeze
the stars clouded the sky,
recreating the moment
when our ancestors first found this place
I twirled under the scattered light,
turning and spinning into the blue

FOR JJ

i remember one sunny day
when dad actually let me
ride all by myself with him
he drove a shiny white convertible
(borrowed or stolen,
no one cared to ask)
he skipped the pleasantries
and went for the green light
screaming past the hardware store
scaring me out of my mind
by driving with no hands

they told him to stop
—and fast, or he'd kill himself
just like i told him
when i was seven
and just like
when i was seven,
he pushed harder on the gas pedal
and laughed.

CHINTZ

mary had these photographs
of famous people
that she cut from her magazines
in her room alone
on friday nights
she hung them on every wall
so wherever she turned
someone she admired
was watching

HOLY

Imagine yourself holy
Imagine the hovercraft
that carts you to the Vatican
Imagine the choirs salute you
the tenors' voices crack
the sopranos fall into
seizures of ecstasy
Imagine the swelling
of your hands the cuticles breaking
the rings shattering
from your fingers
Imagine you breathe
and in breathing
sweat blood from your pores
in some cataclysmic
sangre de christo
fantasy

GOOD

mother you will see me at the airport you will see me
and I won't be giving flowers away or chanting or have
a new hair style and still I'll be there and you will
see that my eyes aren't bloodshot anymore they turned
purple and your cross wasn't replaced by a noose at
all it was just a woven rope because mother I'm flying
away to the jungle or the desert or the next room or
any such destination and I'm not going to buy a house
or rent a car I'm just going leaving parting from what
was my home and I won't come back so it's really futile
to bar down the gate mother it's time it's really time
and we can read the shapes of the words as they flip
through the wheels and I'm going yes I'm going I'm
leaving I'm flying I'm hovering over you like a storm

GLASS

i know this man who lives in a small house
the walls are covered with pictures of his wife.
in his basement, there are hundreds of tiny figures
formed completely from glass
he was an artist before she left
now he gives away these glass men
piece by piece, one by one

POET

I.

I never believed I would write a poem
simply about poetry, simply about
the quality of writing. Poetry is
a god's language, a sacred tongue
I could not know
how to place the words on the page,
how to work with care, forcing the pages
to breathe.
I thought I would never write about poetry,
write about my calloused fingers
write about the weight of the line.

II.

Michael rests in the night.
A green, flickering box shines before him.
Tomorrow is another sick day, another
halted phone call. He thinks about his hair,
the gray peeking out like old produce.
He is glad there are hairs left.
This morning, Michael took his laundry to wash.
The neighbor asked about his daughter.
Michael laughed.
"She is a poet," he said. "She drinks coffee."
Michael cuts his fingers on a butterknife.
The pain shoots in like a burning star

III.

I read the biography of
my new favorite poet.
She has been to Harvard.
She lived in Atlantis.
I read my own biography, twenty years ahead.

In the public restroom, after my first reading,
I search the mirror for prophetic visions.

IV.

Each stone I kick
turns forward in silence.
I look up, spot a burning star,
spot a letter in the sky,
addressed to my father.

I know poetry serves a purpose.
I know poetry is always in solid direction.

I breathe deep,
heavy,
with all air round my body pulling in,
weight myself down,
wade through tomorrow.

CLAIRE BARLIANT

Claire is eighteen years old and Chicago born and bred. Her first poem happened in kindergarten on her way home from school. It was a beautiful spring day, and she found words forming in her mind. When she got home, she made her mother write them down. Since then her mother has been both editor and collaborator.

Her whole family is very supportive of her poetry. Her sister Anne, two years younger than Claire, writes too. "She's good," says Claire—and they're very close. Outside of her family, she feels very shy about her poetry and doesn't readily admit to writing it. "It's hard to be different," she says.

Claire's poetry is very straightforward. This is a quality she admires in her right now favorite poet: Edna St. Vincent Millay. She also enjoys the poetry of T.S. Eliot and e.e. cummings very much, "because of their inventiveness. They make me look at the world in a different way." She reads voraciously—poems, novels, whatever she can get her hands on—and always has.

"My poetry has always been a part of me. Sometimes it is a release. Sometimes it is a photograph in words of something I have seen. To show it to people is to surrender part of my soul."

ROSEATE SPOONBILLS

in the first lights of dawn . . .
                 the rose-colored spoonbill
wakes   s
                e   it s p r e a d s its w i n g s
            s
        i
     r
and
            lu er   of   a   lt   ude
in a gorgeous f tt ing   mu   it
of feathers
                angels   e heaven.
            e   i   r
        k   n   u
they   i   t   z
        l   o   a
       d   a n
     n
    e
   c
  s
all   a

NOW *simultaneously* they   s
                  c
             o
           o
         p
          d
             o
                     w
                      n
                        wards
and d
     i
      v
       e
        d
         i
          s
           r
            u
             p t i n g
        the smooth mirror-like sheen of water.

NINTENDO WORLD

When things get difficult
to deal with,
I take my sister's Gameboy.
If nothing else makes sense,
Tetris does.
The pieces fit together,
But only if I fit them
   cur
ac   ate
        ly.
In this world *I*
am in
control.
But sometimes,
if I'm not concentrating,
I lose,   le
         i   up
and the figures p
on their own will,
no longer forming lines
which disappear
      a
   h   p
but s   e with no consistency
or b   e
  a   c
   l n
    a
Although I try
to move them
        the
out   of   way.
The
  game over game over game over

LEARNING TO DRIVE

I turn myself on each morning,

> (gently release the clutch NOT so fast whew now easy on
> the gas thaaats it ok now we are moving)

Steering through confrontations
I avoid possible conflicts

> (allrightnow put in the clutch and shift to the next
> gear Ack not quite SO hard you don't want to hurt the
> gears)

fearing damage to my exterior
which would confirm my vulnerability—or worse—my strength

> (here is a stop no you can do it this is what practice
> is BRAKE *now* the clutch you're doing fine just SLOW
> letting out the clutch)

Sometimes I feel like just giving up
and my motor dies

> (so it died just start the car again UGH ok keep trying
> you'll get it just remember: make sure it's in first
> gear and reLAX)

Because nothing is more difficult,
than to be left stranded
somewhere
on your own,
standing out.
Forced to be recognized
and to achieve
your goal
without
automatic shift.

11:25 ON A STORMY NIGHT
IN OCTOBER

When thunder, resounding like the Sears tower crashing to the

ground, so powerful, so forceful every car alarm in the

neighborhood cries out like a petulant animal and your house

trembles like it's made of cardboard.

When thunder does that, that is when no matter what you are

or what you've done, that is when you feel like you are the

most miniscule meaningless particle of matter and whatever

is out there could pick you up like an insignificant flake and

flick you off far far out into the universe.

WHAT TO REPLY WHEN
SOMEONE WONDERS

What's wrong?
he asks offhandedly
as I walk by
my teeth locked together tightly
an enameled barricade
restraining a river
of angry answers.
I'll tell you what's wrong.
It's the sun, that traitor, for months
deserting me
for some lonely cloud.
It's the browngreen color
which washes over everything
cats grass people bicycles me
and seeps into the soul.
It's seeing you with
her
and knowing
that if only you were with me,
everything would be
right.

NO MORE ROOM

If I had anymore hate in my heart for you,
it
surely,
    would explode.

And hate would splatter all over the world onto Alaskans and
Italians and Egyptians and everyone else; everyone catching hold of
some of my hate and everyone in the world would hate you and then
some.

Then where would you be?

SWALLOWED BY RADIO

Each word pounding.

Each word striking.

My brain is

giving way

under each

blow.

Too bad my eardrums

can't block the blasts

which cause my cerebrum to
     vib a rate.
And then resound [RESOUND] inside

     my skull.

This noise, it's smothering, PARAlysing me.
a lead blanket.

I wish I was deaf.

Or indifferent.

I wish I could turn it off but now—

I am a part of it.

Not a speaker or dial or antenna

but a sound wave.

Now I do the beating.

ENCOUNTER #3 ON
THE JEFFREY 6

At the rear of the decaying bus
       rich with human fumes,

There is a woman
draped forlornly
           like a damp blanket
                      over the seat.

She looks
up
at
me

as I go to sit
down.

Her bloodshot eyes are
       full of tears.

And her chapped gray lips
       mumble strange incantations
in an unwritten language.

The worried wrinkles are

burrowed into her forehead.

She heaves herself up and exits,

       glancing around surreptitiously.

I lower my head,
trying to push her face out of me,
wishing I could forget.

But she is a part of me now,

She belongs
       to everyone.

THE LAWRENCE EL STOP

The crease in her
      forehead deepens.
As she is struggling
     with the
       heavy carriage and its
     occupant, a toy
         attached for entertainment
   snaps off
      and
         falls.

    She looks up, and her face
        is angry,
        full of blame,
        but it is no one's fault.

A girl sitting quietly
      winces sharply when
       the back wheels of the
     carriage

jolt hard

    out of the train.

LUIS BERMUDEZ

At 18, Luis Bermudez has just graduated from Chicago's Lincoln Park High School. His poetry comes from images and feelings, but is usually cast in a fictional voice. Sometimes the images come in dreams. "I'll wake up at three in the morning. My mother says, 'Turn off that light!' I say, 'Wait a minute! I have to finish.'" He feels the imagery we get is given by God who paints a new picture every day. "I can't believe man or an explosion created all this. It's too wild!" he says.

"My father died in my sophomore year," he says. "He taught me to get somewhere, to respect my teachers, even bad ones. One teacher was always yelling and calling people bigoted names. She and I got into it because of something she said to me about Puerto Ricans. She dropped me that marking period from a B to an F. I kept my mouth shut; if that teacher told me to roll over, I rolled over. I wanted to get my diploma. Getting through high school is a war. I don't see any help for young people. The politicians say there are lots of programs, but I think they're called the Audi Home or Cook County Jail. Everything is black or white. Latinos slip between the cracks."

CAN'T YOU HEAR
THE WHISPERS?

have you seen the blue
images
around Venus' body?
they worship her movements
protect through the storms of fire
never hesitating to strike
yet she turns away
she wanders the earth searching
alone
listening to the whispers of the
wind
they are saying in soft maddening
voices
I love you
coming from all directions
she follows them endlessly,
trying to find the source of her
lover's voice
she crosses the mountains
coming down from heaven's peaceful
arms
into this place where she makes
her home
here she searches endlessly
can't you hear the whispers?

CROW

darkness all around me
did it mean the end? I closed myself
to the outer world opened my inner
eyes
flew away
sweet darkness carried me from place to place
like thick molasses she held me
tight
I picked plumes from heaven's sky
to cover myself
did it mean the end?
she grabbed me by my lockets I didn't pull away in
fear
I became, I shall remain
CROW
the 1 who rides alone
    i
      turn
      2
     Darkness
        with A
        smile

INTRODUCTION TO RADNESS

The visions carried by the winds
        into my wild brain
seductive hands appear they send me to a
freedom to feed off of
only known in the night (owl's hour)
in the waking light I find this
life dull with pain
aimlessly walking through halls
voices rambling, violently gambling
        their lives
    they encourage limbo
where I make my home, I find no hope
Ah . . . finding my elusive night
dig it

        chaos
          A
        new begin

kING

            outside beyond me, there
he sits on his throne
speaking to his subjects, the dirty
nobleman who feasts on refuse. There he
celebrates his hazy state, the heroin kING
"oh loyal friends have we not come
to dance good cheer to all?"
as he tumbles to the ground
little children run to their mothers
mother holds child tightly
"my lord tell us of great battles you've
fought against your own hand"
cries a rat
I was a lad in love with god
replied the kING
till a Kiss befell my arm and
I took my place
this iron spike
became my lord and god
letting out a blunted laugh he began
to cry
I stayed at my place
my wandering eyes remained and
studied his face
rough strong face as if chipped from stone
The movement of his tears
rattled my soul I turned away opened my
eyes. The dream was gone.

LESLIEANN MARIE ANN AND

The midnight
mystery came calling one night in December
the dark clouds were
here to stay
friends never knew her
pain
this little girl always
alone
she lifted a key to open
a door of forgetfulness
always peace there
papa never cared about
the pain just the pleasure
of her legs
mama's soul belonged to a
bottle where the devil
laid.
this doorway brought dreams
this doorway brought love
this doorway brought the end
then one night a scream
came . . .

Her body was found in the hallway
she remained within
her doorway
the only place where she belonged

LOVE

life makes wild love to
death
dancing together hand in hand
naked
rejoicing in fear
in constant struggle
the fire is bright at the
camp site
where these two lovers meet
coming away from the darkness
is wisdom shot into space
for us to grab
wild love is real
we should make love
everyday
wild love, naked dancing together
we'd hold each other
maybe we'd also catch a little
wisdom
I mean love, love, love
love
love
love
      yeah.

RIVER

river the smallest of all great
waters (so alone)
yet can burrow her way
through
live deep within the earth to find
herself pure.
it takes true, gentle hands to brush
away the darkness around
her
to sip from the uncommon spring
is a gift few know
a strange little boy came one day to
find himself
moving the earth
his hand touched her smooth surface
they kissed
he drowned this strange little boy
within her arms
taken by her never to be alone
again

let us not become sullen or cry
death is just another expression
a door to where all truths
are known
here we dance in another truth
our truth

LAST SONG

I got one song
left son.
It ain't new.
I can almost feel the rising
blood.
Oh what's its name:
rebellion.
Shh . . . keep it quiet,
keep it underground.
And then before the man turns to
sip from his wine,
rebellion strikes giving fast
birth to revolution.
Yeah . . .
Can't you see it.
Can't you feel it.
I hope you like my last
song.

VU DANG

Vu Dang is nineteen. He came to the United States from Vietnam two years ago—first to Buffalo for three months, then to Chicago.

Vu Dang likes to study. When his family was in Vietnam he couldn't study because he had to help his mother get food to feed the family—there still wasn't enough and it was not nutritious food. He felt ignorant—this was a very bad feeling. "I came to the United States for my life," he says. "Here I can study, I can learn. I want to make the society better."

How poetry comes to him: he sits on his bed and looks out the window up to the sky. He gets a picture in his head and writes it down. Always the pictures carry meaning within them. Sometimes an image will come in response to a poem he has read. He knows instinctively the difference between a great poem, a good poem and a bad poem by the quality of his response. The great ones, he remembers—not verbatim, but the meaning of the poem.

He writes first in his own language, then translates. He loves his language and uses it much better when he is writing poetry than when he is writing science.

FULL MOON

Isolate
and full, the moon
floats over the house by the
river, the shadow reflects into the house
by the river. At night the cold water rushes
away below the bridge. The bright gold
spilled on the river is never still. The circle
without blemish. The empty mountains with
out sound. The moon bangs in the vacant,
wide constellations. Pine cones drop
in the old garden. The senna
tree blooms. The same clear
glory extends for ten
thousand miles.

THE FEEL OF RAIN

Dampness on neck
spreads, rises from waist.
Hair is jungle's
climate—
Moss-grown wilds
One bird flies past—
A fan's
fiber, shadows of wings
dissolve into a fearful sweep of waves.
The rain comes up in your sleeves,
in the early spring,
and you drown.
The bones of your body scatter.
Your body grows up again
and changes into an angry yet sorrowful
knight rushing towards me.

RAINY DAY

A lover's white bones.   A soggy road in the dust
leads away and back.

The way of a garden.
A pale warrior back from the war
knocks like a stranger, knocks at his own closed
doors.
The garden full of weeds is more silent than in
spring.
More dumb than the rusted door rings.
The word has been destroyed so many times
and this garden stays.
Genial rains, yet too cold.
Lines of silk falling, genial words.

Who gets the whipping?
In the dust there is only the soggy road.

THE ESCAPING SKY

The deadman's face is a swamp unseen by men;
the swamp in the wasteland is the escape of part of the sky.
the fugitive is the brimming of roses;
the brimming of roses is the snow that has never fallen.
The fallen snow is the string being twanged;
a string being twanged is the tear in the veins.
The rising tears are burning hearts;
and burning hearts are swamps, their wastelands.

STRAWBERRY FIELDS
IN SUMMER

Diggers rest beneath trees.
Tree shadows slowly slant eastward.
Searchers of butterfly-orchids are clambering
a snow-white precipice. Forests in the distance
look as if growing in a previous century.
Small birds clamor, like a waterfall
a waterfall without sense of seasons.

And the sun becomes whiter and whiter.
Cicadas' buzz gets more and more on our nerves.
Echoes in all four directions; in them
some degree of primitive sadness.
But mountains and valleys of juicy red
are no longer the strawberries of former times.

MARRIED LATE!

She's eighteen

Married a three-year-old husband.

Every night she carries him to bed.

If it weren't for his folks

she'd kick him out.

The woman next door

nursed her man eighteen years

just to keep her name.

On the third and fourth

the moon has eyebrows.

Fifteenth and sixteenth

the moon rounds.

She'll be old.

She's not like flowers

blossoming and drying.

The moon rounding.

The sun sinking.

WANDERER

```
look-
ing
into
the
dis-        look-
tance       ing                                     a
toward      toward                                  sil-
a           a           a                           ken
cloud-      cloud-      cloud-                       pine
like        like        like            t
silken      silken      silken                  r
pine        pine        pine            e
tree        tree        tree    on the horizon  e   on the horizon
```

```
his         he          stand
shadow      has
small       for-                    stand-
his         gotten                  ing                         a
shadow      his                                                 lo
small       name                    stand-          EAST        ne
            for-                    ing             the         sil
            gotten                                  ward        ken
            his                     standing  to-               pine
      name        but     standing                      t
            he          stand                                   r
      can         a-                                    e
            but         lone                                    e
```

JEANETTE GREEN

Jeanette is twenty-one and is the youngest of three children. She always read: "I inhaled books," she says. Her better poetry generally comes to her in dreams. She has out of body dreams in which she takes on someone else's form and dreams from their perspective; this becomes the stuff of her poems. She also spends a lot of time riding the bus. She sees a lot of things and these, too, are a source of her poetry. "I write kind of scatterbrained," she says, "the way I think."

When she first went to Columbia College, she was blessed in having Achy Obejas as a teacher. "I was brought up Catholic with lots of taboos. There was nothing taboo about Achy. She would have us take off our shoes and dance around the room."

Over the last few years, she has been hearing the voice of her ancestor who came to America in a slave ship. Jeanette figures it may be about five years before the ancestor comes and tells her her story. Until that time, she will have to be content with wisps here and there. I asked her if I should include this in what I wrote about her. "Yes," she says. "Maybe she'll come to me quicker."

SARA NO. 1

One of so few on the first page of the stiffly oldly
new dry
dusted family album.

Sara
Even at three she is lean and delicate and distant.
Tammy at eight is plum-like and a little gooey. And
she can only stare at the picture . . .

At Sara
Dancing before she can count how many times her
small toes will touch the floor.
Sara there with the fairy princess costume
Sara of the little hands
Sara of the pink cheeks
Sara of the curling hair
Sara of coffee cup eyes
Sara of the fire voice
Sara of spirit mouth
Sara of stone shoulders
Sara of darkness spent
Sara of body borrowed
Sara of tight air
Sara of the shallow earth
    how we miss our Sara.

SWEET AND NOBLE

Small
big
Young and gray with knee socks that eagerly sought
ankles.

Face to the walls legs apart.
When he hits her he'll hit her so hard that her
head will knock against the black board, sending
a fine powder of chalk down to dust her hair.
And if there is squirming the little girl hands will
be held and the pulse will echo between them.
One for talking.
Two for talking back.
And much more too many for fighting.
Friday the cuff
Saturday confession
Sunday a blessing!
Go in peace, my peace I give you.
She learned
To knock before entering.
To speak in soft lady-like tones.
She attached sir to the end of her sentences like
jingling keyrings.

In the name of the father
And of the son
And of the Holy Spirit
Amen

BURGUNDY

You so BLACK
You so BLACK I bet that when you go to night school
the teacher marks you absent . . . but tell me where
you've went in back of cornflower eyes

flaxen hair

and pale creamy shoulders.

I've seen you throwin' money out the window for
your little boy to get a ice cream cone.

And I've heard you singing that funky jazz when
you think you all alone.

/If I should take a notion/
To jump into the ocean/

And the ocean welcomed you in sink or swim when
you saw your mothers, your sisters and your friends
bent back.
And their legs forced open by the knees of sailors.
You've grown dim.
You're the night and I've seen you giving birth to
the moon.
I've seen you a mother much too soon,
your little girl tuggin' on your sleeve.
I've seen you with your bible, trying to get me
to believe.
Dancin' for dimes,
fuckin' for nothing.
Your body the darkest
most perfect letter typed on the white page of the bed.
The ink of 1,000 ecstasies
you shadow woman.
Midnight Sister.

GIRL

Women of my house
I haven't voice for more
than a whisper. It's Mother.
She's thrown the mourning
cloth over her head,
and neither sound nor touch
will wake her.
My sisters we are she
while we walk the soil
and the Man/Dog is killing
us.
We are run like birds through
the grass.
There is no one to call
the spirit smoke.
No one to feed
the dead.

SHADOWS

Summer cotton spinning, almost all gone.
Draped like shed skin around your dancing body.
The sting of the mother warnings gone from the swell
of your body.
Half-blinded by the music
distracted only by your dance.
You didn't hear me smile at the slow dip and grind.
The slight opening of the door bringing to life
the passion of sight.
Can you dance?
Your hips swaying with the breeze of your breath.
A flush of blood neon through your veins.
A lover's (me, my) kiss bright on the amber carvings
of your breasts.
A black thread of hair caught by the sweat of your
efforts beat a swirling path on the cushion of your
stomach.
The quiet moon your belly-button hung nearby.
For me would you dance?
If I offered you violets or soft lady-like applause? The
thigh of one reaching to meet the thigh of another.

I turned from the doorway remembering the water
of your hands pure on the stretched earth of your
body. The sheen on the inside of your pillowed thighs
bright with the
light before the dark can consume.
My eyes burning from looking to the sky to find the
sun when I was told it was only in the fire.

UNTITLED #5

This is not the woman who covers her face in her sleep.
Who pulls on mittens during an October dusting of snow.
She bakes our bread, the flour filling the lines of her hands.
She turned her head when my nephew's arm was cut and
    dripping blood.
Clicking a light dim and off in a dark room.
That woman stayed in bed for the night.

I hear the bed groan and cry a little in the night.
The faint hum of breath and the snap of broken sleep.
The boxcar shuffle of slippers leaving the room.
I'm left only with the sound of falling snow.
And the crackle of ice freezing in my blood.
And I know she can kill him with her bare hands.

If I can talk to her, maybe hold her hand.
It always gets so bad at night.
I should never have let her leave the room.
I shouldn't have let the hurt pile and drift like snow.
I shouldn't have let the killing thought seep into her blood.

The soft knock of his hand on the door to her room.
The fist twisting her arm to pin back her hand.
The white undershirt washed and bleached snow
white in the Mickey Mouse night light night.
The being told to shut-up and to go to sleep.
She remembers her nine-year-old thighs smeared with blood.

"What kind of beast does that to his own flesh and blood?"
She screams from the kitchen. The sound echoes in the room.
"When I was eleven, I tried to go three days without sleep."
She tries to button her coat, the knife gleams wicked in her
    hand.

"I'm going to do it, I'll walk all night
I don't care if I have to walk in all this snow."

Then she leaned on my shoulder, her tears burned and cooled
    like snow.
Her eyes burned so red they seemed to swim in blood.
I held her fast and eternal and sure in her night
gown.   Standing with her coat buttoned wrong in the middle
    of the room.
The Sears carving knife hanging heavy and limp in her hand.
In this dark it's really me who needs the sleep.
"I gotta get some sleep, which one of us is gonna shovel that
    snow?
Your hands are so cold, drink some tea, it'll warm your blood.
I'll straighten the room, I'll bring you a little something before
we call it a night."

WIRE-RIMS: 1936

The black drape of her hair fell into her eyes and
she pushed her glasses up.
She ran along the halls barefoot and sliding on
the polished floors.
She sat behind the water closet door laughing, laughing
into the curling cup of her hands until her wrists
were wet with tears.
He wouldn't find her standing so still with her
mother's cotton dresses and her father's Sabbath
Day suits.
She crept away from the slow heartbeat of her lover's
footsteps.
She shrugged the blouse from her back and her skirt
collapsed willingly at her feet.
She let him catch her in the cold-pantry.

And his hands were on her like rain water in the
tide.
Steam pouring from the slick and tang of her body.
He pulled the cold glasses from her face and kissed
the blindness to her.

1943

The world ripples flexes cringes

Her glasses wait cold for her on the loose puddle
of wool and cotton at her feet.
Her shaved head nods in the clinging snow and a
thread of urine spirals down her leg.
She covers the twin tents of her breasts with her
hands.

When she sees her MarMar she will tell her to check
the oven, MarMar something is burning . . .
She hears a train coming, a shower would be
good
clean.

EDUARDO AROCHO

Eduardo Arocho, twenty three years
old, is in his third year at Northeastern Illinois
University. He is studying the teaching of English
in secondary education and Spanish. He is proud of
his Puerto Rican heritage and speaks Spanish, but
he wants also to be fluent in the written language.
"I want to know the formal," he says.

Eduardo wrote his first poem in September of
1992. "It wasn't very long ago," he says, "but I've
been preparing for it all my life. You never know
what you have until you discover it. This poem was
a love poem to someone I couldn't have. I never
read it at performances—it's too personal. Everyone
withholds something for themselves."

Eduardo is a shy person. He wants credit to
go to the people he's written about, not himself.
"I am just the medium. God gave me a gift. It is
my job to write their stories, not to bring credit to
myself. [Puerto Rican writer] Piri Thomas said,
'Words can be bullets and words can be butterflies.
My words are bullets and butterflies.' I agree
with him."

BETTER THAN THE MOVIES

It was
a summer afternoon
And it was
the sun
that lit our view
And it was
a day to spend
with friends.   And there was
                 sun light
                 camera eyes
                 and action
                 from a hand gun.   And it was
                                      at the corner store
                                      And he laid
                                      on the cement floor
                                      And it was
                                      the neighbors
                                      that gathered to see
                                      he   that   was
                 And it was   fourteen.
                 his cheek
                 stuck on the street
                 And he had
                 three bullets
                 in his back
                 And he was alone
                 with no mother
And it was   to cry good-bye.
the police that came
and it was
one cop that smiled
and said,
"This is better
        than the movies."

EMPTY LOT

Empty lot
our summer park
void of all green
and swings
where once a house stood
where little
Puerto Rican boys,
Mexican boys,
African boys
and poor white boys
play the games
of the street.

Empty lot
between two buildings
in the middle
of our block
filled with gravel
and rocks
bricks, broken bottles
and all kinds
of human junk.
Where only weeds grew
and funny brown things
that stuck to
our shoe strings.

Here we gathered to play
all kinds of games
like baseball,
softball, football
and dodge ball.
Sometimes we had
stick fights

and sling-shot wars.
Here races were run
and "IT" was played.

Empty lot
where one afternoon
a gangster got shot
his mother ran
to the lot
to cry
her last cry
for her son
as our park
was stained
with tears
and blood.

Here is where
little boys
play
from morning
till dawn.
As they grow up
they stop playing
in the lot.
Some move away,
some stay,
some become gangsters,
some just vanish,
but always
the memories remain
of those summer days
when the little boys
played
in the empty lot
our summer park.

THE WARRIORS OF
A GHETTO LAND

There they stand
the new warriors
of a ghetto land
freshly ousted
from their homes
by a crabby welfare mother,
an alcoholic father,
a pregnant sister
and a dead brother.
No school today
cuz the white teacher is a pain
it's safer in the corner
with the new family
Calvin, Juan and Chico.

Protecting their hood
against the gangbangers across the street
and against the police.
On the side
selling and getting a little "high"
fucking the girls in the neighborhood
is better than selling burgers
or fast food
working the night shift
night after night
waiting for those "knights"
who dare cross the lines
Calvin has a sparkle in his eyes
it sez, "I want to die,"
Juan has a furious look in his eyes,
it sez, "I'll never die,"
Chico has a peculiar look
it sez, "I'd like to be a doctor one day."

In the nearby street
the sounds of a boom, boom beat
it's a car with a loud system
and it's coming full speed.
It stops at the corner
a window rolls down
and a hand pops out
it makes the sign
of the other side
it's too late
for the warriors' escape
the car speeds off
their bodies fall
a pool of blood
is their bed
on the cold
and dirty curb.

There they lie
the dead warriors
of a ghetto land
Calvin, Juan and Chico
in heaven, alas
another Puerto Rican,
another Mexican
another African
killed by their brother's hand
all that remains
is some blood stains
and their names
on the wall
R.I.P.

ACTRESS UNSEEN

Actress unseen
too shy
for the stage
too bashful
for T.V.
She prefers
the living room
with an audience
of just two.

Actress unseen
her comedy is surly relief.
The T.V. is on
yet all eyes
are on her
as we watch her
jump around
and yell out loud
mimicking us
in pixillating scenes
we fall
to the floor
laughing inordinately
at her goofy countenance.
Forgetting the miseries
of the day.
It's a wonder
how burlesque
life can be
at the edge
of poverty.

Actress unseen
her tragedy

never forgotten
a gangster's gun
has taken away
the life of her brother
she loved more
than any other.
Even today
when she tells
that tragic tale
that would make
even the most austere
man cry,
tears flow irrepressibly
from her eyes.
No script
to this
real performance.

Actress unseen
playing with her large family
as a cast
her nieces and nephews
she loves,
her mother
has strength for all.
Her lover
gets a private showing
of the lovely
Puerto Rican
primadonna.
Then at dawn
the same routine
work hard
all day
till the curtain
closes.

"BANG," "BANG"

"Bang," "Bang"
I wake from my sleep.
Is it the fourth of July?
No, it's war in the streets.

"Bang," "Bang"
kids play with guns
it's not a toy, it's the real one
and that's real blood.

"Bang," "Bang"
the vehement cry outside
a mother's baby died.
It's lasted all night!

"Bang," "Bang"
who was that boy?
Why did he die?

"Bang," "Bang"
revenge is sweet.
The war is perpetual,
so no one sleeps.

TRIAL OF MISS AMERICA

(Post War Trial of Miss America, Rainbow Shoes Part VI)

Miss America
is on trial today
The people
are the jury
God is the judge
and everybody is watching
on T.V.

Miss America's
face looking grey
with a cold grin
hanging on her
face
as she raises
her right hand
to say,
"I Do"
to tell the truth
no bible needed
for definition
cuz God is present
and he is truth.

Miss America
is on trial today
The judge says
let the prosecution
begin
and everybody
is watching
on T.V.

Miss America

the evidence
is clear
you are accused
of kidnapping
the black man
seducing
the brown man
at the red man's
home.
With thousands
and thousands
of bottles of
gold liquid.
As they drank
your liquor
the empty bottles
encompassed them
like a prison
and they forgot
about their women
and their children.

Miss America
is on trial today
she pleads
not guilty
for reasons
of insanity
and everybody
is watching
on T.V.

Miss America
while the men
were imprisoned
by your liquor,
you stole their
green and blue

land
and forced their
women to work
for you
while you abused
their children
and erased
their fathers' names
from the books
you made
then you teased
them by giving them
guns
to play with.

Miss America
is on trial today
her finger prints
found all over
the place
a decision
has been made
and everybody
is watching
on T.V.

Miss America
The judge sez,
you have been found
guilty
and before I read
your sentence
your punishment
won't be as expected.
No execution
or life imprisonment.

And the people

yell, "Foul
for justice!"

And the judge
sez,
"No, that would
make you
just like her."

No.

You will be
compelled
to give back your
crown
and stop making
books.
And you will be
condemed
to tell the truth
of your crimes
for ever and ever and ever . . .
on T.V.

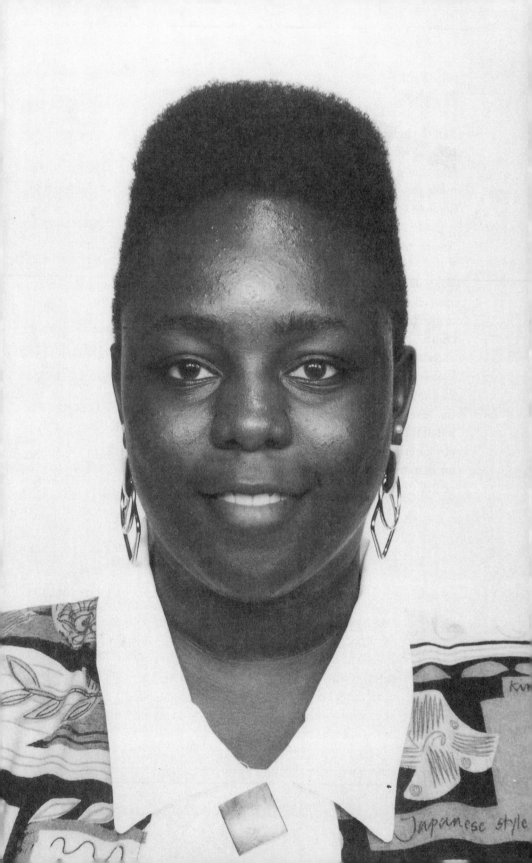

ANDREA WREN

Andrea is twenty-four years old. She grew up in East St. Louis, then went to Spellman College, an all black women's college in Atlanta. At seventeen it was her first time away from home and she was excited—although initially also sad—to be going, exploring another city. "It was intoxicating and empowering to be in this all-female culture." Maya Angelou was required reading there. It was at Spellman that she had her first exposure to poetry—at first, through reading. "I read and I read," she says, "and pretty soon I wanted to write." There was an event at the school that had a great impact on her life: A Tribute to Black Women Writers. Gwendolyn Brooks came, and Sonia Sanchez, Toni Cade Bambara, Pearl Clay, and a host of others. Andrea was mesmerized—most of all by Sonia Sanchez. "I loved her message, and I loved her words, and I knew I wanted to write like that."

Why does she write poetry? "If I didn't get stuff down on paper, I'd have it all roaming around in my head and I think I could really go crazy. I understand what Alice Walker meant when she said she might kill herself by the age of thirty if she didn't write; just walking around seeing everything that's happening is enough to make you lose it. Writing gives me peace of mind."

THE SCREAM KEEPER

i am dark—
darker than despair.
i am my people's midnight.
i stand quiet in my darkness,
silent in my pain.
my tears are suspended
as stars in the sky.
i am the keeper of secrets,
the garbage can for dreams.
i have listened to the screams
of the victims of murderers, rapists,
drug dealers, gangs;
victims killed by the hand
of their own arm.
i heard the pleas for help
but i am helpless to respond
for when the night was invented,
it was given no voice.
i am the keeper of screams,
an abyss of lost dreams
i am my people's midnight.

THE RUSSELL-CITADEL

the newspaper-rugs would rustle
beneath his slow gait

he spent hours musing over
stacks of books
writing a square palmer method
of notes onto paper

"that's all she wrote" he would say
when the money for candy corn
was exhausted

his salve
for my split finger
was listerine

i grew with 3 generations
of male wrens
in that blue shotgun house
on russell
non endangering
or endangered
endearing . . .
they took care of me
in their sanctuary
from the women
and their eau de-toilette
women smells
and voices devoid of bass

grandaddy had woodsy smells
a soft tattered voice
a daintiness of hand
coaxing greens, peas

and watermelons from the land

he would share the harvest
with a knit of neighbors
with his son and his son's son
and the candy-corn eating
son's daughter

RASHEEDA'S ACCOUNT

"That Bitch Set Marion Barry Up"
a slogan for t-shirts at the time.

he's been under surveillance
for years . . . me, for months

found myself on the other side
of the law
agreed to the plea bargain
instead of depending on the
blindness of justice

i thought about
what people would think
him in an expensive hotel
with a woman not his wife
and that "just say no" bullshit

hell, it won't spoil my career
i haven't been on the cover
of *Essence* since the 1970's
but i will be on the cover
of *Newsweek* and *USA Today*
photographed in limousines
with my best tailor-made outfits
clinging to my still slender body

anyway, i offered him the pipe
would have let him blow me
if it wasn't for the audience
'cause i still care for the bastard

people will mistake me for
a judas-bitch
a race-betrayer
i was simply looking out
for rasheeda
and rasheeda's own

when i kissed his cheek

OFF BROADWAY

we were watching "Spunk."
at intermission, i saw you—
the most beautiful black woman
i had ever lain eyes on:
sovereign grace,
small salt and pepper 'fro,
and frozen toffee for skin.

i wanted to tell you
but i was scared
to approach.

15 minutes elapsed
during which i performed
a back/forward dance.

finally, you walked our way.
i got in step:
whispered "you are absolutely gorgeous"
then walked away.

FINALE

and there was fire
and the people ran from e. st. louis
across the river
horrified you ran all the way to paris
trained your feet to dance instead of fleeing
listened to "the intelligence of your body"
and the parisians fawned over you, showcased
your poise and glamour in elaborate silver cages
and exotic poses
you ready to pounce, purr
roar or mate . . .

show after show
pet leopards and furs
the needs of the rainbow tribe

america's rejection . . .

you wondered about leaving your mama
and sister in such a heartless land . . .

then katherine dunham and her troupe
put a spell on you, inspired motion
in those feet again
and you danced
learned french more fluent than english

and who will ever forget the pictures of you
on the steps of your chateau
in a blue shower cap and robe

once again you had no home
you had to put a balm on the chords
decorate your face and soft body

with thick makeup, false lashes
and grandiose costumes:
no longer able to fit
into that scandalous banana skirt . . .

and after the song and modified dance
you transfered the makeup to cotton balls
took off the feathered headdress and gown
laid down surrounded by roses
tiger lilies, morning glories
echoes of "encore"

WHOLEHEARTEDLY

for hank gathers

you were probably
NBA bound. the basket
ball your ticket out

of poverty and
your mother a fair home. your
heart slowed you down. you

stopped taking pills. you   r
could execute unsedat   a
                                                   o
                                             s

                              mount
ed now.   d   a   s   h

you gave the dunk the
whole of your heart. how the crowd
roared as you took off

FRANCESCA ABBATE

Francesca Abbate is twenty four and an only child. When she was eight, she started writing poems to entertain herself. She was shy and didn't have many friends. The poems made her feel like she was talking to someone.

She is now among the mountains of Montana at the university there, studying with Mark Levine for her MFA in poetry. "The mountains just sink into my poetry," she says. She loves it there. She knew before she went how it was going to be—that it would be right for her.

How she writes: A line comes to her that has an idea in it somewhere and "I have to find it. The poem is about finding the idea." She takes the line and writes as much as she can from it. "I began believing in a place," she says, "an internal spiritual landscape in which there is a different sequence of events, a different space and time." This internal landscape changes as to whether she's in the city of Chicago or the mountains of Montana. The more places she goes to in reality, the more the internal landscape changes and grows. "When I'm writing from there, I know it's right, it's where I'm supposed to be."

AFTER THE ART INSTITUTE

The sun spars with us, two broad hands blocking the way—
the el wedges itself between buildings whose windows
have been blown out by the light, stacks of matte black squares
the cars are a brittle hurtling over glass tracks, over a river of tin.
We cross into the edges of the city, where the sun is stuck in a spasm
of self-reflection, struck blind over the butchers and liquor stores,
blind over the billboards that face lots where weeds grow
into trees, where boys disappear by the hundreds
with their habits, checking into rented rooms, into rooms
the women can't visit.

It is too much light: locked in my belly in a steel box, a time
capsule whose catch will open like a bullet. All day
we have been playing dangerous in the museum, searching for maybe
selves along the walls. You are a Spanish soldier with a seal-colored
mustache, a glass of wine, a pipe in one red hand. I have less
to choose from: the virgins with their faces held slantways to the sky,
like books left out in the rain—their own faces, texts they've never
read. Instead, I find the inevitable still life, show you how the split
ruby of the pomegranate glistens, how the grapes in their wood bowl
are a jade clearer than water, celadon worlds of frost, mouths
that have had their words flushed from them. I tell you the honey
treetops in the forest are where the catwalk of the heart lays hidden.
Before we leave, you insist on finding Van Gogh's little room, midnight
drawn through the window for the color of three lone walls, for the bed
and nightstand. I watch you make up the fourth wall as you look, you
and your always body.
The frame is thick, the frame is what tells you what's painting,
and what isn't.

The el knocks us together. Our faces stare from the glass as if some
shattering has flung them into the far white sky: they float back, but
never close enough, having grown used to such distances. Desire
is a room with a blind floor and a glass ceiling. You know this.

Every second we are busy building rooms we can't live in:
the fourth wall, our bodies, are not stone or oil or canvas,
not clay, though we mend each other with spit,
like potters mend cracks.
We will never be nostalgic: this light will break us, this sky-poison,
this sun that swells up bigger every year over all these bodies
out in the city, at the edges, in the projects: we can't pretend our
lives are any different—we too will split, be buried, and this light
will go on, a bridge that has always been burning
by the time we got to it. In the heat, the refraction of sweat on our skin,
the rocking of the train, mindless, catching our bodies pitch, we learn
to ask our questions silently: where desire is,
where the rooms that will not have us live.

LANDSCAPE

You take me out of the city at first snowfall
the light from the high road a thousand blurred candles
and a scattered red beating like hearts held up
to floodlights, the cars below
a dull wave calling witness, passing.

In Arizona, the orange trees in the cemeteries
had mouths dug so hollow
there was only room left in them for the word end.
I drove by thinking few of us would ever find
ourselves, thirst driven, into a grove like that;
the oranges burned hard by years of moonlight
the only juice our own need to strip them down
to stone pits and ash. Below us a siren

snaps the dark in raw hands and trails the seeds
of its burst season with it.
The view from this rise is milk-sad, the town laid out
before the mountains, the buildings no bigger
than the hunched red knuckles of a card player
set patient at a table. What happens between people
happens in all five directions: the black hills
and the same dark trying to read our faces.
On the way up the storm pulled back
from the car, opened for us like those white
cemetery blossoms, the hollow parting of hands
to water. In the valley

there are churches with white faces and black
roofs that were built for this climate, they have hips
as stiff and pale as ours. Our lives have brought us
to love the dark grace of churches, and grace itself
which is the color of glass in a black river.
Night could hold the span of us in just two fingers.

HUNGER STORY

A woman strews bread crumbs in her hair
and walks out into a field, her figure olive brown
against a landscape of wheat, her arms finished
at her sides, done. When the crows

come, they will lift so many strands
of her hair in their mouths
that from the road she will look like an oil
medusa, she will look like any woman
who has tried to wrench herself
from the headache of guesswork;
from the body, which asks so long
of itself, so much.

The moon comes up, drags the black
cape of night behind it. She thinks
the moon is the corner of a house
with all its lights left on, the corner
of a house where people wait
and wait. In the dark she keeps
happening upon herself, a room left
in a hurry and come back to a stranger.

Dawn is a scraped down blue, the static
hum of the sky rushing to piece the picture
back together. She speaks to it, she says:
Love, your mouth tastes like vinegar.
There is bread in her pocket
for breakfast. It is enough.
It will all be plenty.

CRUMBS

My mother has a cup and saucer face.
She takes a spoon from the dish rack,
presses its backside to her forehead and says:
Honey, count to ten.
From the coach house I can see just
the tips of the lemon trees, and behind them,
the wind pushing a passage of grey hills
further into the distance.
Someone in the house is cooking breakfast.
I run my thumb over the green side
of a lemon, hear egg shells crack,

the coffee maker hiss. Last night
I wrote the boy's name on a piece of paper
and let it fall to the grass.
I hung Chinese lanterns from the gutter
over my window—now they brush
against the house, pink and pale blue
and mint green. I take a piece of stale bread
and rip it to bits for the birds in our garden,
watch the big ones struggle to fly
with their thumbnail wings. Up here, the trains
sound from two directions at once, part
call, part echo: after-noon means the sky
is dark with grass. I go back

to the kitchen. I eat what's left of the bread
and write how good it is. I count the words
in my hands—here, the word full, then:
milk summer mosquito lemon. I add mouth
to one palm, bread to the other. Now
my mouth is a word in my hand
and I put it to my lips.

Now mouth, now bread. No-one's home.
I finish dinner, sit on the back step

until I hear my mother say
Tell me something. She's standing
in the periphery of the kitchen,
a plate in each out-stretched hand.
I kick moths up from the grass, think:
smoke, horizon. My ankles itch.
When she's gone, I go to the garage,
take the two good ladders
and lay them crossways on the front lawn,
white wood looking out on green grass.
I step back towards the house.
The hills turn blue, then small.
I can't believe how small the hills get.

FOUR POEMS

Farm

Night is the quiet interval of bird's
buried heads, their wings half-hearts
and blacker, strung on long wires
in a sleeping country. I leave my boots
on the stone porch pointing home.
The June bugs are heavy
drunks too tired to get past the screen.

Even my hands are sunburned.

Stop

I was saying something. It was on my hands
like water, or better, a windshield loaded
with rain: my hands were glass and I was about to
break you and time bent this way, and the same color
as T.V. The sky's been turned up all the way to white
white as the spit-lines where the creek catches
and drags on stone. The wind blows the dead
center of a pink rose wide and casual near the water.
Tell me what I can't remember.

Letter

No one tells any stories over and over.
The marquee near my house reads LOVERS
in block red letters. I think I have made them.
I think I have built the alphabet because it is more
familiar than anything I've done.
When I pass the theater I say to myself:
this is how men are this is how women are and
in the country of winter every marquee reads LOVERS.

I can see them passing, the peculiar cast of each
set of shoulders and their eyes
heading up past the yellow sign
and into the palm of night, the grave
moon set there. Everyone's fucking everyone else
and it keeps getting colder.

Green

There are checked curtains in the kitchen and I sleep
at the table. I am dreaming
I put my hands flat on your chest, thumb and forefinger
breaching each black nipple. I am dreaming of kites
I can't pull down, then I wake up working the field
again, only it's mine. The house
smells green. The doors are gone
and the sun comes so low the cat jumps its tracks.
Everyone is happy as matches.
I step out into morning and everywhere
the petty kindness of grass.

SPELLS FOR EARLY WINTER

one
The body is a town like this one,
so far from any other,
making such quiet choices.
Today the sky is grey backed
with white; the light just tips
the mountains, those good-hipped women
laid down and not going anywhere
soon. Birds open overhead
like a spasm of black umbrellas
coasting into rain. I keep thinking of winters
in a catalogue of cities, of snow
easing out the dug rows, the black-
yellow strips of Wisconsin fields.
The prairie got blank when it came,
the few trees stepped back white
into the pale of sky. We'd drive
for hours in those two colors, cupping cigarettes,
the heavy wool smell of the car's heater
and the cling of smoke
on our cold fingers.

two
I take my hands
try to show you how it is, how
the house came down last night
and I don't know the way
to put it together.
This morning, done washing the floors
I opened one palm down on the wood
and waited for the light to reach me.
When it did my hand was full of wet
and the sun slipping around on my knuckles,
those five tough stars.

I hate all this, hate how life comes
at me some days the way children round
a corner running so hard the wind
might take them for birds about to come apart
and all in the shape of white, of flurry.

three

Take the child out of the house.
Bury him in the field. Cross
the ground with the sole of your shoe
twice, toe to heel. Say:
I love nothing so much as this good round blood
in the bowl of my belly, this bowl with one eye
still on the ache of the saw. Go inside.
Take all the bottles and tip them
bottom up from the lips of the drains
until they've wound down or dried.
Hook the spit from your mouth
with one finger.
The blood comes like rain, irrational, still
and on all night.
Now try love without thinking of knives.

four

Night lays fat in this house, turns the moon-glanced
windowsill to chalk. I can feel the step-ladder
of my ribs rising in me, this aggregate of bones
and thin chance. Listen, I've forgotten how we make
the same gestures over new each time.
I've forgotten what my hands mean except lately
they are full of the sound of dark, the hollow pulled
from a drum. I wish you would stop teaching
me to myself. I wish I could lay my arms out
on the kitchen table and stretch the cut-me lines
of my wrists out to face you
because I am sick of these worst sins.
Alone, the mirror says *Woman, I still
call you mine.* I don't know who to believe.
I don't know which one of us learns.

LOT'S WIFE

1

This is how the summers go, in the ecstatic reach
of the sunflower, the broad orange that grins the lost
round oh's of the season, their coarse green stems raw
against white garages or leaning out from ditches
like women just got up to say goodbye

2

From across the caught fire of this autumn street
you are a stranger, you and the man who is always
on the corner with his bible, his doomsday lips.
Why question the innocent? All week-end
you have been talking about Lot's wife
how she must have led them out
of the city. You keep asking me how Lot
didn't look back, how he kept on walking. It's the old
voices again; winter, which is the color of salt,
crying don't leave me, don't go anywhere I can't.

3

We've taken the rocking chair out to the porch,
cups of coffee, a few books. The four o'clock hand
of the sun scuffles behind my ear, one rough
thumb on my neck, a beat like wings
lingering on the pulse of my skin.
Close your eyes.
I want to say this sad thing out loud, that last night
you were a coat I could wear, a coat whose tag read:
Girl, it's bad luck to wish for a name you can't go out in.

4

I assure you,
we'll be the end of us yet.
I don't know whose
eye you are looking for in the storm, only
that you keep going into it
with your just short of hopeful
hands and your own eyes averted. Listen,
I would gather all of July if I could, the white
scratch clouds, the pollen, their bees,
the dragonflies
and smooth it up on the window of a train
so that we could travel in one sustaining note
of blue passage. This light, which is already
echo, is the last good light of the season.

THE PLACE WE COME TO

I would rather a country forgetting
night and heaven
where forever lodges in the throat
a desert whose stones hold mirrors
to sky

The afternoon burns on all day
and women burn and the men
they touch too burn
touch meaning fire ants and honey
wood fingers with slit-eye knuckles
that see the way the pressed mouths in trees
that limbs have been cut away from
see

Flies do not drag their black
wings through morning
and we have stopped pretending
each day is a new world